RawDuality

Jermel Cook

BookLeaf Publishing

India | USA | UK

Presentation by *BookLeaf Publishing*

Web: www.bookleafpub.com

E-mail: info@bookleafpub.com

ISBN: 9789360944681

First edition 2024

I dedicate this to my late grandpa for his commitment to helping me become the man I am today. And to my daughter for continuing to bring about growth in me. Both for my well being, and to better serve as her first navigator in this world of ours.

ACKNOWLEDGEMENT

I would like to thank BookLeaf Publishing for this opportunity. Thank you for giving me a chance to potentially put some of my words and passions into the world.

PREFACE

Within these verses, you will find moments of profound introspection and moments of transcendent bliss. You will witness the juxtaposition of light and darkness, as they intertwine and shape our understanding of the world. You will feel the bittersweet embrace of joy and sorrow, and the tender ache of love and loss.

Through the power of words, this collection aims to evoke a range of emotions and provoke deeper contemplation. It is my hope that by immersing yourself in these pages, you will find solace, inspiration, and a renewed appreciation for the intricate dance of opposites that defines our existence.

So, navigate this labyrinth of emotions and explore the connections between seemingly opposing forces. May these poems serve as a reminder that in the delicate balance between light and darkness, joy and sorrow, love and loss, lies the essence of what it means to be human.

Morality in gray

I've always contemplated direction in my life.

the what if factors

what if my life continued the path of its origin

what if I hadn't learned the ways of a pacifist
over activist in the grimiest narrative

what if my middle namesake carried its origins'
weight through me rather than my rejection of
its ways.

in another life I'd have been darker, harder,
someone the me today would not know.

This current and its turbulent flow

The blessing to my life surrounded by survivor's
remorse for what I used to think should've been
my demise

It taught me duality through the lens of life

That we are not more righteous nor despicable
beyond choice and consequences of our own
plight

The road to hell is paved through good intent
and I've born witness through my own morality
as it ascends and descends life's traversal.

Through good and evil in waves from people
painted in grey

 Highlighted through our narrowed eyes tilt
towards perspective views guaranteed to sway

There is no clear view in humanity's structure.

Only flaws that life exploits. And through said
narrative. we are both the hero and villain of our
tales through the eyes of the next narrator.

The perfect weapon/ Humanity's Duality

What is this path I found myself on, filled with unsure thoughts, wild feelings, untamed, waiting to cut through the surface

Like claws full of anger, tension, desire. Such a pure destructive sensation, I was born the perfect weapon.

Confusion riddles my thoughts, fueled by adrenaline rushing from this primal feeling to escape, have I been lost

I'm often overwhelmed with life, so much pain, lost and sorrow, the innocence in me fades with every trial, what comes with tomorrow

Never certain what turn life will take next but always sure there's more to be endured, the future is never sure

But still I'm expecting to endure with faith
Without something to ensure

Forsaken as I fight, because life always rewards
me with ties that shackle me to fate, fate
destined to destroy me and all that I put faith in

Lord what does it take

What does it take to persevere and fight without
victory in sight

How do I sound

Do I sound spoiled by you, for questioning faith
in the ability to see something better in sight

Don't know how I sound

But what I do know is this anger within me, just
as pure as what innocence remains, what do I
hold onto, would one break me while the other
persevere, or do they both make up who I am

Two half's believed to birth prosperity as well as
destruction as such their design

I hold both love and hate

The ability to give and take

The perfect weapon

Born of an unshakable fate

Through whatever fuels my hands command, I
can lead this world to greatness or its ruin

This perfect weapon is human

Inclined to your light

Can I be transparent with you. Truth is I feel
alone most of the time. There's an underlying
itch I can't scratch in the underlay of my mind.
Most days I can play off my overlay and
announce that I'm fine. And on surface levels
most days I'm really able but my spirit can't
deny

That I'm still searching for better purpose than
simple purpose in being present in this present
day society of normal unnatural conformity my
soul bleeds

I long to share often, long to love long day and
night because on most days the intensity of my
underlay only subsides under the physical
pressure of guilty pleasures, one of humanity's
many vexes my biggest one is S.E.X

Because as physical as this process to procreate
may be it still stands to reason that this
Sacred-Energy-eXchange is still our most basic
form of spiritual to soul connection, it's the
easiest lesson we ever learned as simple

adolescents despite our conscious mind
unsuccessfully grasping its connection

And yet when it's all said and done I still fail to
say I need you, because I learned through past
pain and rejection to implement pride to cover
pains residuals

So now I'm here, seeing you in my dreams my
last great burst of unexpected euphoria, and the
lingering feeling that until I remedy this
blockage of generational deliria

I can never feel freely, without judgment, stifling
emotional block or overflow, and the need to
experience love and connection through sex
when I need to just feel you and let you feel me
organically
I can't see

stonewalled till it catches me, Blue balls at
emotions peak, Even with erection, it humbles
me
To focus on something better to better me

Hoping to eventually bridge at peak

The connection I seek, still starts with me...so I
still strive for self-discovery to be present when
it finds me

Reconnect with me at love's peak

Plus 2

Can we start over again, not from scratch, but
experience, not reactive when things are tense,
but proactive before we bend

When life makes us agitate, can we still walk
with faith in each other's care when so much is
on our plate

I got so good at walking away, cause when it
hurts we question if it's worth the stakes

It takes to maintain

Raining heartaches

Echoing pain

Life's a bitch and it frustrates

But we can withstand the change

Alone we strain but together we have range

Not in oneness but unified bliss, not we but us,
two wholes with shared trust

We feed each other's energy

Shared synergy

Vibe endlessly

Love make relentlessly

I crave this kinda intimacy

Cause it robs hardship of all its intensity

I'd wait an eternity for its divinity

Channeling Duality

Our vicious cycles... My dualistic rival
We are two halves of one whole's equal

You manifest my demons
While the pacifist has always been my
appointment mission

You hold my fears, the ugliness I hide away
I uplift my strengths, and the tenacity to never
sway

You are the rage, the guilty pleasures of the flesh
you crave
I push for peace, in search of worth beyond the
physical tease

You are the evil, I seek to defeat
I am the good, and you'd love to see me
deceased

But you are my strength
When I find my resolve weak

You are the drive
When I question the consequences of my design

You are the survivor
When I feel like I'm drowning in heavy waters

You are the wrath shadowing my peace
I am you
You are me

I fear you, but I need you. With you I'm a whole
issue for whatever issues life issues.
Imperfections to match my life lessons. My
darkness to compliment my light's visage

There is Harmony in you and me

Our roots

Love love we all love, it's a part of us

To trust love is to cultivate love, it's marvelous

We speak, eat, sleep, bleed love, in life we trust

So why love, so hard on us, we're broke enough

life teaches hate when at its base love was its
birthing place

we fear love because love hurts but real love
mends the worst of us

Our trials and errors are simple growing pains

We're scarred and that's fair cause we're human

but every solution is taken care of when we
chose love first to prepare us for life's
adversities

Please trust and believe I know heartache and its
reach is deep, seeping, seeking to destroy all
peace but still it's necessary to release that

negative energy, believe in its possibilities and
you'll see.....love is peace, granting serenity

Empathy

You say it's love's effect

I say it's repetition
You say our hearts connect
I say we got shared visions

You believe in hearts that mingle when met

I see connection when mindsets on track

I know at our core we are not the same. But all
in all we share each other's pain.

It's strange cause it feels like I've loved you for
many moons, sunny days or rain. It's brand new
even when I think your ways are strange.

You comfort me when I'm in pain, I push you
when you can't maintain. We love one another
with deep range though we come from separate
worlds, sometimes I can't explain

But

It's simple, hearts mingle no matter the issues,
opposites do attract so it's safe to say we have
been proved

our connection and tenacity to break through the
lies people tend to spew about what's
compatible. I know the truth

yes me and you, we are the proof that you can
love from beyond what's you, what you know
and what you been through

that glue that mends what you can't see through
when you are in its brew.

That's you to me and me to you. I'm the
practical wall, you have emotional glue but it
takes two to mingle. I'm happier than I ever was
as a single soul, and I feel you are too, just as I
know you feel me too.

Somehow empathy paved the way for me to
finally see someone like you

Simplicity and complexity

Our complexed selves

Collectively we believe in status over self.

First impressions and material wealth
Not much stock in faith or health
It's amazing how we ever find the space and
time to love ourselves
Ridicule and peer pressure is what we learned in
our time of youth
But that shit transcends decades and takes space
overcoming truth
The old stick with traditional ways some grand
but some still come from them slave days

It's crazy cause Nas once said all that gray
meant you'd seen something, know something,
so you ought to have something of worth to say.

My vexes came from lessons of betrayal of the
heart, rejection and residual scars. They manifest
to my guards, harder than jail bars, when my
heart flinch, it don't make sense how we love to
fight love but still want someone bold enough to
break down our defense. We invest in a

temporary fix to curve our internal mess. Fuel up
on this world's medicines, drugs, and toxic
weapons of generational wasted space, faith in
ways that never saved men.
Why must we waste away.... When the heart still
craves, what the ego takes away. If we would get
out of our own way. I guarantee we'd find a way.

But alas still complexed, my generation's
complex. My heart is complex. We want love
but fear the reject. So we find comfort in our
mess. Till we get restless and reset.

Still trying to get it right, that's our duality.
That's our plight.
We are the last generation who knows of the old
fight but can still influence our future's
collectively new life

So I pray this message transcends our complex
ways that someday we as a people might
simply...find a way

Lustful drugs

Careful of your type.
Cause I get lost in your type

With emotions deep enough to swim in

I crave the waves of your curves in motion

So high off the notion of pleasure in our time

During the time of our prime

It feels like your mines but our generation values
the decline of a commitment bind

So for now we lay up, fuck and get high enough
on lust to call a stoner's bluff

As the sweat drips
And I'm immersed in your lips

It's clear we're not in love
But the intensity of this trip
We could never get enough of

Transparency

How often do you find yourself surrounded by
so many familiar faces, yet feel so outta place

Trust I've spent the time and know that phase

Isn't it amazing how feelings for just one soul
could fill that whole space

If you believe in such a thing as past lives then I
am certain your presence influenced mine

A haven for the heart, we lay intertwined

Peep our divine structure built to find balance in
one another be it body or mind

When your presence meets mine it's a
celebration to blend

With our souls blessing we tend to the wounds
of life we're given

It's that sweet release that draws us in when we
need to mend, if we came in pairs then I'm
certain

The image of me reflect you, and vice versa
must be true

As I come to find me, in turn I'll see you

Wounds and soul ties

Trying to find balance in you
It's a fool's errand true

But truth is this addiction is proof
That I'm drawn to the beauty beneath your
chaotic roof

Dependant on one another's aura we find fleeting
euphoria

Mending these wounds of self-sacrifice in the
name of love lost
Layers created to guard the heart I thought

That no one could see the truth in my scars but
here you are

You saw through my facade with simple sight
without judgment or doubt

And for all your flaws and dependency of my
presence I'm invested in the innocence of your
visage

So fragile in fear of relapse

You cling to a reason to exist in peace and
choose me as a safe haven

For one fleeting moment in time, at the lowest
point of my heart and mind, to find another just
as wounded as I, is like a blessing in disguise

Before our union's demise. I just want to
internalize how it feels to connect in our darkest
depths

Our wounded soul ties

Turbulence

I've been here many times before, seeking
serenity in peace in my spirit when the mind and
body wage war

Usually sure I've got the answers for all I seek,
but resolve is where I pitfall. Fighting the
absolute solution trying to find a route where
everyone wins... even if I lose

Rinse and repeat I've spent my young life
purposely choosing the short end because in my
mind, I was resilient enough not to break so why
not bend. As life trickles away, perhaps self
sacrifice as selfless as it implied, really is my
biggest sin though my heart still denied

But I've revolved this plane of existence now
three decades at present and the tide is shifting.
Anxiety peaks as the dam of indecision gives
way to a certain level of clarity and self
repentance.

I want to receive what I've given. and give more
in true abundance. Not from an empty cup

spread thin but residual love born of something
reciprocal and true.

I welcome this turbulence as life does not flow
consistently and fixed, nor can it be controlled as
our ego cannot dictate our own lives' flow, only
mirror and adapt its rhythm's tempo

I want to flow, so ego...must go

Where faith and doubt, share space

I heard that my mind was a beautiful place to traverse. At a time that my spirit played in limbo unsure I was worthy since my past carries stains I'm ashamed of

I heard tonight that I deserved true love from a life long love I once thought I'd spend a lifetime with in love, being laid to rest because even love is not enough of a sustainable drug

I witnessed a soul who once broaden my perspective on soulmates being plural and not just the ones you mate with, but those who reflect you and the you of many paths we can traverse through the flesh while still kindred to each other, sharing the same space

Find her way out of her own way, developing before my own mind's eye but alas in this reality our time had already passed and the flesh felt doubt when the time came to congratulate her success, I hope the soul understood what my heart couldn't bear to reprocess.

I have been keeping faith at war with doubt.
Regurgitating my past trauma in cycles to
reevaluate my past rivals

Pain, lust, anger and doubt

At each pivotal point of my own developing
pace, still trying to out-pace me as the flesh only
grows weary of this world while the spirit
sharpens to empower my overall resolve.

Pain created gratitude

Lust taught me where love could and could not
be.

Anger, is only the reflex to avoid sadness when
you cannot smile and be happy

Faith and doubt are always one, never too far
past the thin line we fabricate to avoid being
broken

Duality is why they exist together in these
moments we create to cope with our vexes

Shared space...
To give our reality shape

Dopamine

So much creation in the brain constantly, it's no
wonder my anxiety won't let me sleep.

 Like a hype Melody

Get to writing, exercising. Rehearsing vocal
notes or sketch the beauty of her mind's eye
rising

It's ironic cause it's a rush of wonder when I
accomplish these test of my creative schemes to
better vocalize the vexes of my being that
otherwise feeds on lust, caffeine, drugs and
artificial beings

Yeah that's a mean rush like CRANK when they
hit his heart with that cocktail drug, had him
twisted

But we misfits take to the streets in quick fits to
get hyped up quick

Feeding the buzz that we millennials don't know
what living means, when baby bombers and gen

x came first on the curb in some ways worst so I
heard

We only followed the word a mouth and half
stepped our way into this trap too brazen for self
doubt

Hella doped on life's greatest vexes, can't curb
that ex cause that sex was the best, weight lift
for that natural gain, cause anxiety rains so
heavy that a joystick and virtual reality is the
only safe haven where every reward shapes the
cravings for that quick "pat me on the back
cause I did that" sensation

Heart attacks and blood sugar on the rise at the
tender age of our prime because what's right for
us has been monopolized to those more wealthy
than us. And these radio waves from our cellular
plugs keep us turn up on the ultimate drug of
thumbs up and artificial love from artificial love
through a portable screen of unfamiliar fans
from the hub.

What's the real buzz

Wisdom got harder to find when information got
easier to get without life lessons

So we drowning in depression overload cause
the POWERS THAT BE steady finessing

From the time of our adolescence we been
surviving cycles of old times meets the new

The last generation that could tell you the truth
that when we came this world was falling from
the need to instantly rise

As a result it's been left up to us to save the
world from its dopamine high

Driven

These days my past time peace time is on the
road, vibing through my mind's eye.

Reminiscing on all my past lives, of a time of
arrogance, spells of ignorance, the tempest of
my adolescence

Iridescent when in view of my reflections

I enjoy the thrill of the highway wind as I look
down my vision once tunneled by the mission, to
be enough, for myself and my indecisions. For
those I loved and their mishandles of my love's
provisions.

Gifted in empathy's wealth, I remember how I
would drown myself, it's liberating how much
I've freed myself.

So much so that as I tread this pavement I can't
help but reminisce....my God, I've fought so hard
for this

Fallin

Products of love hurt then make us stupid,
reckless, obsessive with who we lust with.
Steady trying to connect with

Cupid still sniping, we still falling for jaded
missions, till we start numbing it from over
usage of love's drug refurbished.

Can't move forward for fear of losing. Feelings
can be so ruthless
Learning to empathize just to have it starved,
cause you over sympathize when no one can see
you through your own eyes. "How many times
will you sacrifice yourself for a world that will
never love you as much as your love's true." She
asked. Offering her love, selfishly yes. But deep
down, yearning for me to save some love for my
selfless vex. "Till I change the world to
something I'd be happy to send my little girl into
without fear of her pearl being tainted by these
visions of hell I see in spells." I replied,
superficially pleading for my self-destructive
tendencies to put love before me. Sacrificing so
much of me to see a better way for life to be.

Can't blame me for a belief in how love should be received. But can't afford to love me because it's just not realistic living for the world we live in. And she could not follow for a lack of believing

It's a lonely mission for something meant to be passion personified in its meaning

But what's real takes real sacrifice to believe in

So silly me for believing in love fallin....

Conflict/ the perfect weapon, pt 2

From physical, mental, to spiritual

I've been at war for balance since my first born physical

Craving balance in a world constantly tipping its scales on an axis that has long since lost its way

Yet and still I find it pivotal

To feel it all

Yet remain symmetrical

Every fleeting emotion gives way to some manner of humane understanding that our conflicts are our only form of resolution

From simple children fighting for toys that we want cause we want it, no solutions

To the wars we wage for the sake of lands, rights, and privileges we believe is ours to claim and hoard, in the name of our revolutions

In every form of our need to be seen

My need to be needed

Your need to believe in something unseen

Our need to exist, we persist because we need it

Our humane arrogance

 It's equal capacity for penitence

Perplexing my spirit in waves as I contemplate
what it means to step above it all in my current
existence

To manifest the best of what we pray for,
meditate and seek to channel while we exist on
this plane

At every transition of my own self-awareness, I
contemplate my existence. And my answer is
always found in the gray...in duality's haven

Humanity's duality, are we the perfect
weapon..or our own salvation

Only our collective conscience might provide
the answer to that question

PAssION

Pain is within passion

lately I've felt it in waves, pure attraction

Creating has become so much easier to imagine

fear of failure seems inconsequential, a stepping stone in every action

Inevitable

As I dig for something within, aching and pulling at me for freedom, I pursue what's conceivable

Is this what it means to be consumed by your inner dominion

All I see is depth around me

All I feel is death within

At the mercy of this intimacy

What becomes of you as you lose innocence in
the face of life's turbulence for all to see

Pops, would you be proud of what you see

You once told me I was too innocent for the
world around me

But would you be happy now to see it fading in
me

Or would you take pride in how I channeled my
pain, sorrow, rage.... Into something you could
better Understand

into something our world could do more with
than reprimand

For better or worse, balance is demanding its
due from within

How much more before innocence is no more
and I've poured it all on life's canvas for all to
see

Will there be any redemption for me

I wonder what my guardian angels see

Do they weep as they witness the death of me,
give way to depth in me...

She is

Loved Queen I don't mean

To objectify your beauty, believe there's no scheme

But if I may appreciate it for all it means

It puts me in the mindset of a most divine being

Captivated by your melanated features

Pretty brown eyes like mother earth, I love to see ya

Smile with such a vibrance, you'd swear the most high designed it

Pretty dark brown locks or thick curls, I appreciate the textures

And your lips. Just a kiss could send me over the moon, sweet bliss

I digress. I love every inch of your beauty, trust there's no gimmick

I could go on, but you get the message

Because every inch of your beauty could be described as a patient design featuring every perfection. You see imperfections. I see lessons in beauty in the eye of the beholder's perception. My lesson was acceptance and I'd gladly accept it to be in your vicinity. Yes you are the epitome of beauty in its simplicity, giver of life. I could speak on it day and night, but let me not objectify the... Beauty of your melanated heritage. I simply want you to get the message, a lesson in love and appreciation for your visage

Dear queen, for you this is my message... Titled- She Is

Worth

Do you assert yourself in self-empowerment or outward dominance.
Is your worth determined by the popular status quo, or do you get high off personal ego.

Is it as fragile as paper weight or dry wall. Or can it stand tall from life's pitfalls and stone walls when opportunity withdraws.

Some base their worth in the same category as faith. "As he who strengthens me" is all it takes to move mountains when times are hard and decisions have high stakes.

Me, well. My self-worth like many has had a rollercoaster of stages from low to high, high to low. Mighty lows thanks to ego, and the most high thanks to generational faith. You know how the church goes.

But still I've never been able to shake this feeling that there's more to one's self-worth than their accolades, faith or status. I once wrote that your name held little worth till you took action that mattered.

And that still matters today. Not a status on a page. Not one accomplishment that you gas for days. Not a verse that you preach on replay till people's ears bleed, like how Sway.

I mean personal self-status accompanied by many milestones, failures and developed good habits.

Self-fueled

Self-sustained

Your own rules

Your own claim to fame

I believe to conquer self is to conquer life metaphysically and the like, every visionary's delight is a world built off personal insight to encompass it. Because that is our natural right.

I grew up not able to see myself or my mission, sense generational curses often left me with clouded vision.

So when I speak on this, my self-appointed mission is always to strike with conviction.

Because to have life is to value it and you must understand that yours is no different.

Then he, her or them it's forever a fight within to be authentically you but that trial by fire is the best one to win.

Conquer self

Hero

I want to be your hero
Because I've felt this feeling of powerlessness in
place of hope

Feeling the desire to protect. To save someone in
need, in pain...in distress... In their darkest resets

Unbearable to see.
With a little heart of hope
Just wanting to be

Can I fight for you
Against this void

Till you yourself
Can find your joy

I know
How it feels to be low
With no where to go
Like no one understands our sorrow
Waiting to implode

I can't let go
Powerless to change

But eager to go to blows

A hero
For those whose hearts know sorrow

I'd bear it all... just to see your smile glow